Explorers
& Traders

This edition published by Barnes & Noble, Inc.
by arrangement with Fog City Press

2005 Barnes & Noble Books
Copyright ©1996 Weldon Owen Pty Ltd

Published by Fog City Press
814 Montgomery Street
San Francisco, CA 94133 USA

Conceived and produced by Weldon Owen Pty Limited
59 Victoria Street, McMahons Point, NSW 2060, Australia
A member of the Weldon Owen Group of Companies
Sydney • San Francisco • Auckland

WELDON OWEN PUBLISHING
Publisher: Sheena Coupe
Creative Director: Sue Burk
Managing Editor: Rosemary McDonald
Project Editor: Kathy Gerrard
Designer: Jill Ryan

FOG CITY PRESS
Chief Executive Officer: John Owen
President: Terry Newell
Publisher: Lynn Humphries
Production Manager: Caroline Webber
Production Coordinator: Monique Layt
Sales Manager: Emily Jahn
Vice President International Sales: Stuart Laurence

Text: Claire Craig
Illustrators: Paul Bachem, Kenn Backhaus, Nick Farmer/Brihton Illustration, Chris Forsey,
Tony Gibbons/Bernard Thornton Artists UK, Adam Hook/Bernard Thornton Artists UK,
Christa Hook/Bernard Thornton Artists UK, Janet Jones, Steinar Lund/Garden Studio,
Martin Macrae/Folio, Darren Pattenden/Garden Studio, Oliver Rennert, John Richards,
Sharif Tarabay/Garden Studio, C. Winston Taylor, Rod Westblade
Maps: Steve Trevaskis, Mark Watson

First printed 2004

M 10 9 8 7 6 5 4 3 2

ISBN 0-7607-5916-2

Color reproduction by Mandarin Offset
Printed by SNP Leefung
Printed in China

A Weldon Owen Production

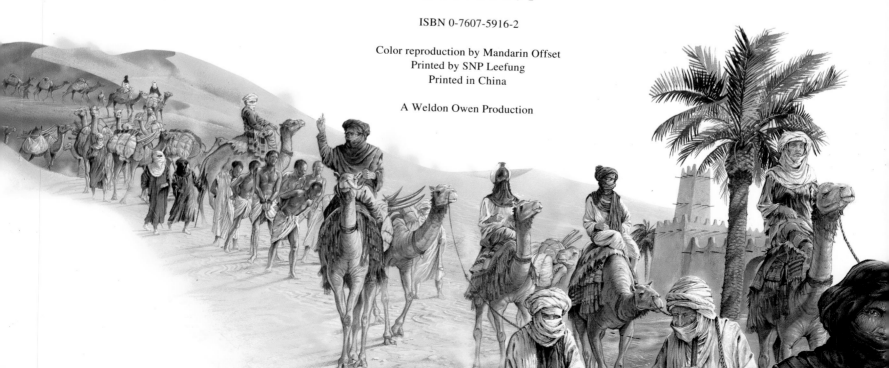

DISCOVERIES

Explorers & Traders

CONSULTING EDITOR

Dr. Anne Millard

Department of Environment
London, England

BARNES
&NOBLE
BOOKS
NEW YORK

Contents

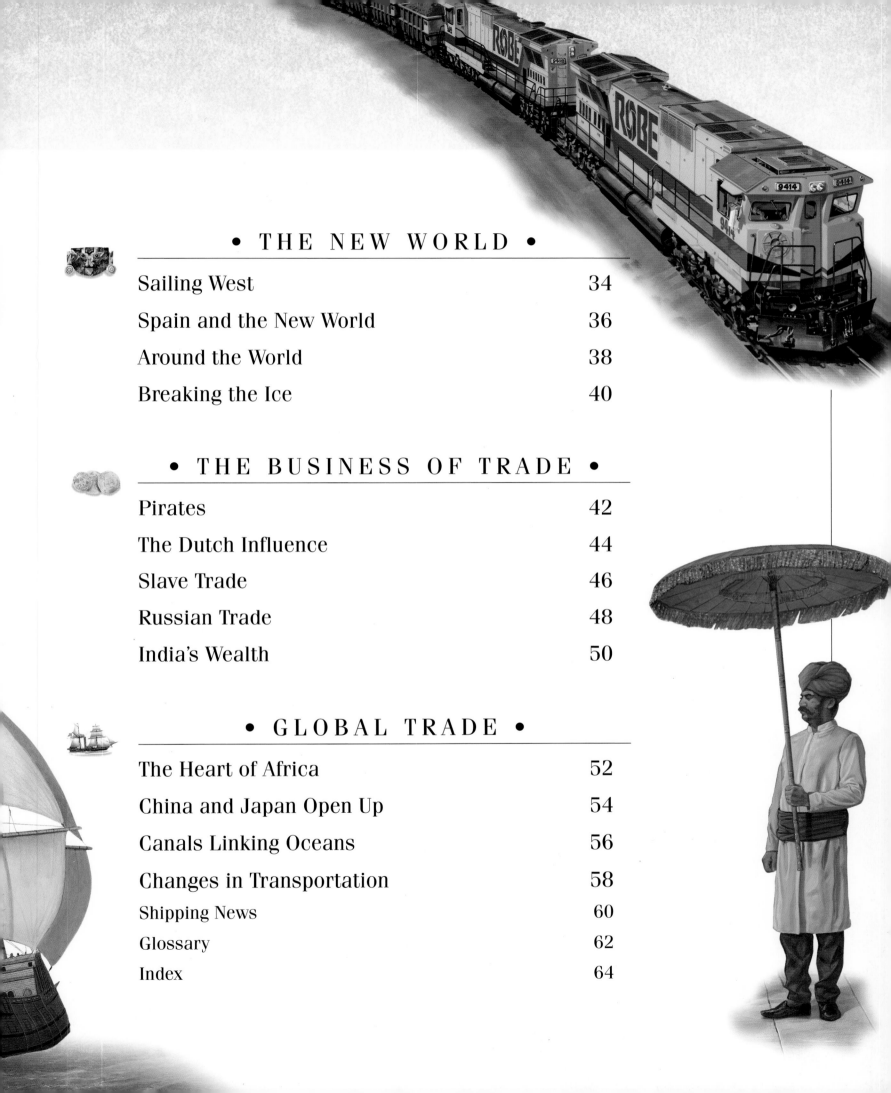

Early Trade and Exploration

The world looked very different 20,000 years ago. Great glaciers, caused by an ice age, covered much of the land. The people who lived at this time were hunters and gatherers, and they were always on the move. They followed herds of animals; gathered wild nuts, berries, plants and shellfish; and fished the rivers. They traveled long distances for things they valued, such as flint for making tools and weapons. Gradually, they drifted across much of Europe and Asia, and crossed into North America. At the end of the last ice age, around 10,000 BC, the glaciers thawed and lush forests grew. As the climate changed, so did the way humans lived. Many continued to hunt and gather food, but people in the Middle East planted crops and bred animals. They made pots, wove cloth, and used metals such as gold. Soon they started to trade with other villages for goods they could not produce themselves.

PAST REFLECTIONS
People made utensils and tools from obsidian, a black volcanic glass that was highly valued. Almost 9,000 years ago, women at Çatal Hüyük in Turkey used obsidian mirrors such as this to put on their make-up.

FLINT AXE
Hunters used bone or wood to chip flint stones into tools with sharp edges.

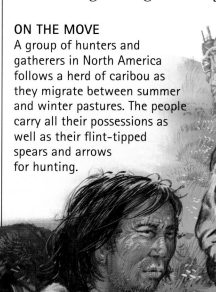

ON THE MOVE
A group of hunters and gatherers in North America follows a herd of caribou as they migrate between summer and winter pastures. The people carry all their possessions as well as their flint-tipped spears and arrows for hunting.

SURVIVAL TOOLS
Hunters and gatherers caught their prey with weapons such as wooden daggers with deer-horn points (far left), harpoons made from wood (middle) and spearheads made from deer bone with flint set in carved grooves (left).

GOLDEN BULL
This bull made of gold came from Bulgaria. People often traded for precious metals, such as gold.

WORKING THE LAND
Early farmers in the Middle East made the first plows and harnessed oxen to them. Thousands of years later, this farmer in central India uses similar tools to plow his land.

Q: Why was flint so important to hunters and gatherers?

VILLAGE LIFE

The town of Çatal Hüyük, in southern Turkey, is one of the oldest towns in the world. People built these mud-brick houses, which were joined together and entered through the roofs, in 7000 BC. Some of the houses were special shrines, decorated with wall paintings, for worshipping the gods. The people herded cattle; grew wheat, barley and peas; and were skilled clothmakers. They had plenty of obsidian and exchanged it for goods from other areas. Çatal Hüyük soon became a busy trading center.

Discover more in Sailing West

The First Civilizations

The first civilizations, Sumer and Egypt, flourished beside great rivers between 5000 and 500 BC. Sumerian villages prospered on the flat plains watered by the Tigris and Euphrates rivers, while the flooding waters of the River Nile left fertile silt for Egyptian farmers to sow their crops. These large societies organized their resources. They developed irrigation systems to direct and control the floodwaters, and store them for later use. They invented the plow and the wheel, which they used for chariots and to make pottery. People made laws to govern society and developed their knowledge of subjects such as mathematics. New groups in society, such as priests and skilled craftspeople, began to emerge. The Egyptians and Sumerians exchanged local produce at regional centers, but they also traded outside their own countries for goods they needed, such as timber. They began to keep records of their trade, and early systems of writing developed. The first civilizations were large and successful. They were the basis for the way society is organized today.

JEWELS FROM AFAR
Trade in precious stones gave Sumerian jewelers new materials to use. This necklace is made from lapis lazuli from Afghanistan and carnelian from the Indus Valley.

ROYAL SKIN
Egyptian royalty and priests sometimes wore the skins of exotic animals. Princess Nefertiabt, shown here, wears the skin of a leopard.

TRADE LINKS
Sumerian and Egyptian traders often made long and dangerous voyages. They obtained goods from India, Afghanistan, Crete and Greece. The Egyptians also traded with Punt.

FOR THE QUEEN'S COURT
The Egyptian Queen Hatshepsut sent a trade expedition down the Red Sea to the ancient land of Punt. The Egyptians here are loading their ships with frankincense trees, elephants' tusks, ebony, gold, spices and exotic animals such as panthers.

WIND POWER
By about 3200 BC, the Egyptians had invented sails to power their boats, rather than relying on oars. This enabled them to explore further for trade.

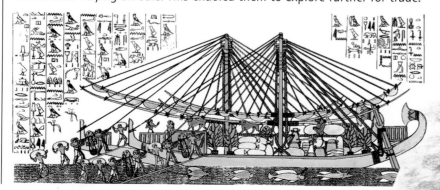

WRITTEN WORDS

Ancient people inscribed pictures on stone and clay to record events, actions, or details of trade. This stone tablet is a very early example of record keeping in Sumer. Its pictures show how much grain was traded. Pictographs, however, soon became more abstract symbols. The Sumerians developed wedge-shaped cuneiform (from the Latin for "wedge") characters, which they wrote on clay tablets with a pointed instrument called a stylus. The ancient Egyptians wrote on papyrus or inscribed their tombs and temples with a picture writing called hieroglyphs.

Mediterranean Trade

The Phoenicians were great seafarers and traders. Around 1000 BC, some set out from their cities on the Lebanon coast to find new lands to trade with and farm. They filled their ships with goods such as carved ivory, glass and cloth that they dyed with purple ink from the murex shellfish (left). Sailing west, they established trading bases in areas that were rich in metals, such as copper and tin. They supplied King Solomon with cedars from Lebanon for his temple in Jerusalem, and the Egyptians with timber to build their ships. These excellent navigators also made the first known voyage around the coast of Africa. The Greeks began to trade in the Mediterranean around 800 BC. With olive oil, pottery and wine, they traded for grain, timber and metal along the northern shores of the Mediterranean and the Black Sea. They also ventured down the Red Sea and sailed on the monsoon winds to India. By AD 110, the Romans had an enormous and wealthy empire that extended into North Africa and the Middle East. They traded only for exotic goods, such as silk from China and wild animals for circuses.

SILVER EXCHANGE
This silver Roman cup was found in Denmark. It may have been traded, given as a gift, or taken as a prize of war.

TWO-FACED VASE
Trade with other countries gave artists ideas for their work. This Greek vase, from 540 BC, shows two of the different races of people in the Mediterranean.

MAPPING THE MEDITERRANEAN

The Greeks and Phoenicians sailed throughout the Mediterranean setting up trade colonies. Because they were rivals, they usually settled in different areas.

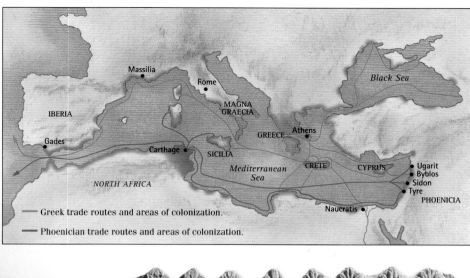

— Greek trade routes and areas of colonization.

— Phoenician trade routes and areas of colonization.

ROMAN SPORTS

The Romans obtained most of the goods they wanted from their own empire. But they did trade for wild animals such as lions, which their gladiators fought in the great amphitheaters.

SMALL CHANGE

Small silver coins appeared in some parts of Turkey as early as the seventh century BC. King Croesus, the ruler of the ancient kingdom of Lydia, introduced both silver and gold coins, such as these, into his realm. A standard system of money made it easier for different countries to trade with each other. When Greece began to use coins, each city-state made its own and stamped them with special symbols. Coins from Athens were stamped with an owl, the sacred bird of Athena, the Greek goddess of wisdom.

Discover more in The Silk Road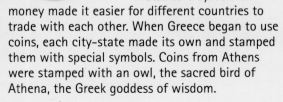

Arab Traders

By the ninth century, Arabs were trading extensively by land and sea. They sailed down the east coast of Africa, and caught the monsoon winds to India. Arab traders even reached China. Merchants roped together camels, donkeys, mules or horses and traveled over land in Asia in groups called caravans. They also crossed the Sahara to the gold-mining areas of West Africa. The Prophet Mohammed, the founder of Islam and once a merchant himself, approved of honest trade. Merchants were very respected, and tales of their adventures were the talk of the markets. Some of the stories in the famous *Arabian Nights* tell of merchants and magic carpets, awakened genies and mysterious places. The busy market of Baghdad in Persia was an important meeting place for traders from Europe and Asia. European traders brought furs, cloth and manufactured goods; Indian traders brought gold, jewels and spices; and there were slaves from many nations. After much bartering, traders returned to their own lands laden with goods.

LOCAL TRADE
The Arabs made pottery plates with beautiful glazes and colors, which they traded in the local markets.

AN EYE FOR A BARGAIN
Merchants, such as these from Turkey, checked the merchandise carefully. They bartered and haggled for hours to get the best price.

HEAT AND DUST
The market of Baghdad was a maze of narrow, dusty streets with small, dimly lit shops on either side. Huge canopies deflected the fierce heat of the sun. Different streets were set aside for different goods. Here, the carpet sellers' street meets the spice traders' street.

THE POWER OF ISLAM

In the seventh century, the Prophet Mohammed founded the religion of Islam, which means "submit to the will of Allah (God)." Arab traders carried Islam with them into Africa and across Asia to China. Followers of Islam are called Muslims, and they read the *Koran*, the sacred book of Islam, for advice on how to live their lives. Muslims pray five times a day, facing the Holy City of Mecca where the Prophet Mohammed was born. Every Muslim tries to visit Mecca once in his or her life.

SPREADING ACROSS THE SEAS

The Arabs conquered a vast empire, which stretched from Spain to Persia. They set up trading networks along the eastern coast of Africa and across the seas to China.

SAILING THE SEAS

Arab merchants sailed in vessels called dhows. With lateen (triangular) sails to catch the wind, these ships were light and fast. Many dhows are still built as they were hundreds of years ago.

The Vikings

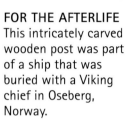

FOR THE AFTERLIFE
This intricately carved wooden post was part of a ship that was buried with a Viking chief in Oseberg, Norway.

INTO THE EAST
Viking traders discovered the wealth of the Middle East in the ninth century. They traded for goods such as this gold statue of Buddha.

The Vikings were proud, skillful sailors. They fished and traded in Scandinavian waters and farmed the land around them. But as the population grew, farm land became scarce. Toward the end of the eighth century, Viking explorers left Scandinavia in strong, swift ships to see the world beyond their jagged coasts. The Vikings from Sweden sailed to eastern Europe laden with walrus tusks, ivory and furs. They set up trade routes in the Baltic and bartered for silver, pearls and Chinese silk. Early in the tenth century, they ventured along the great rivers of Russia to the rich markets of the Near East, such as Baghdad. The Vikings from Denmark and Norway sailed to western Europe. They stormed towns and looted monasteries, and Europeans feared the sight of the fierce Viking warships. The Vikings conquered some of the lands they raided and many settled down as farmers and traders. Others crossed the Atlantic, where they discovered Iceland, Greenland and the New World.

A BOOTY OF SILVER
Silver buckles, coins, necklaces and bracelets were part of a hoard of tenth-century Viking treasure discovered in England.

GOODS FROM RUSSIA
The Vikings traded with Russia for slaves and luxury goods such as delicate silver arm rings.

EASTWARD TO TRADE
Viking traders row their knorr to the shore of the Baltic coast to find a camp for the night. During the tenth century, Swedish Vikings traveled along the Dnieper and Volga rivers and traded for silver, bronze vessels, pearls and Chinese silk.

VIKINGS ABROAD
Vikings from Sweden traveled east to trade. Vikings from Denmark and Norway went west to invade and settle new lands.

A VIKING EXPLORER
Erik the Red, the famous Viking explorer, discovered Greenland. His son Leif Ericson, shown here pointing at land, explored the North American coast in AD 1000. He and his crew spent the winter in what he called Vinland, which may have been Newfoundland.

ALL AT SEA

The Vikings built superb wooden boats that were strong but light. They used small fishing boats for local trade. The wider and slower cargo boats (knorrs) had shallow bottoms so they could come in close to the shore to be loaded with goods and livestock. Raiding parties traveled great distances in sleek, fast longships with shallow hulls. The Vikings named them after spirits of the wind and the sea and carved their prows with fierce dragon heads.

Fishing boat

Knorr

Longship

Across the Pacific

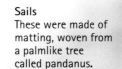

The Pacific Ocean covers one-third of the Earth's surface. Small islands are sprinkled across the enormous blue expanse and often isolated from each other by great areas of sea. The islands that make up Polynesia (meaning "many islands") were settled by seafarers from Indonesia and Malaysia, who spread gradually across the Pacific looking for new lands to settle. Between 2000 BC and AD 1000, they navigated incredible distances in sturdy dugout canoes, reading changes in the swell of the sea, the patterns of the stars and the easterly winds. They brought with them a patterned pottery called Lapita (above left), which has become an archaeological clue to their movements. The settlers adapted to the different environments they found, from the dry atolls to the lush and fertile volcanic islands. They reached Tonga and Samoa by at least 1000 BC and developed their own customs and a society that was ruled by chiefs. By about AD 1000, Polynesians had reached the easterly islands of Hawaii, Easter Island and New Zealand.

Sails
These were made of matting, woven from a palmlike tree called pandanus.

DID YOU KNOW?
Gigantic stone statues line the coast of Easter Island. The people carved these guardians of the island from soft volcanic stone, then dragged them to platforms on the cliff edges.

SEEKING NEW LANDS
Polynesian settlers sailed across the Pacific to New Zealand, which the Maoris call "the land of the long white cloud." Their double-hulled canoes were loaded with fruit and vegetables, such as breadfruit and sweet potato; pigs, chickens and dogs; and crops such as taro, yams, bananas and coconuts.

READING THE SEA AND THE SKY

The Polynesians were expert navigators. They found islands to settle in the vast Pacific Ocean by "reading" the sea and watching for land-based birds such as frigates (above). They traveled to and from these islands using maps they made from palm sticks and cowrie shells (left). The sticks represented the swells and currents of the sea, while cowrie shells marked islands.

Paddles
These added to the power of the sails. The Polynesians steered the canoe with the back paddles.

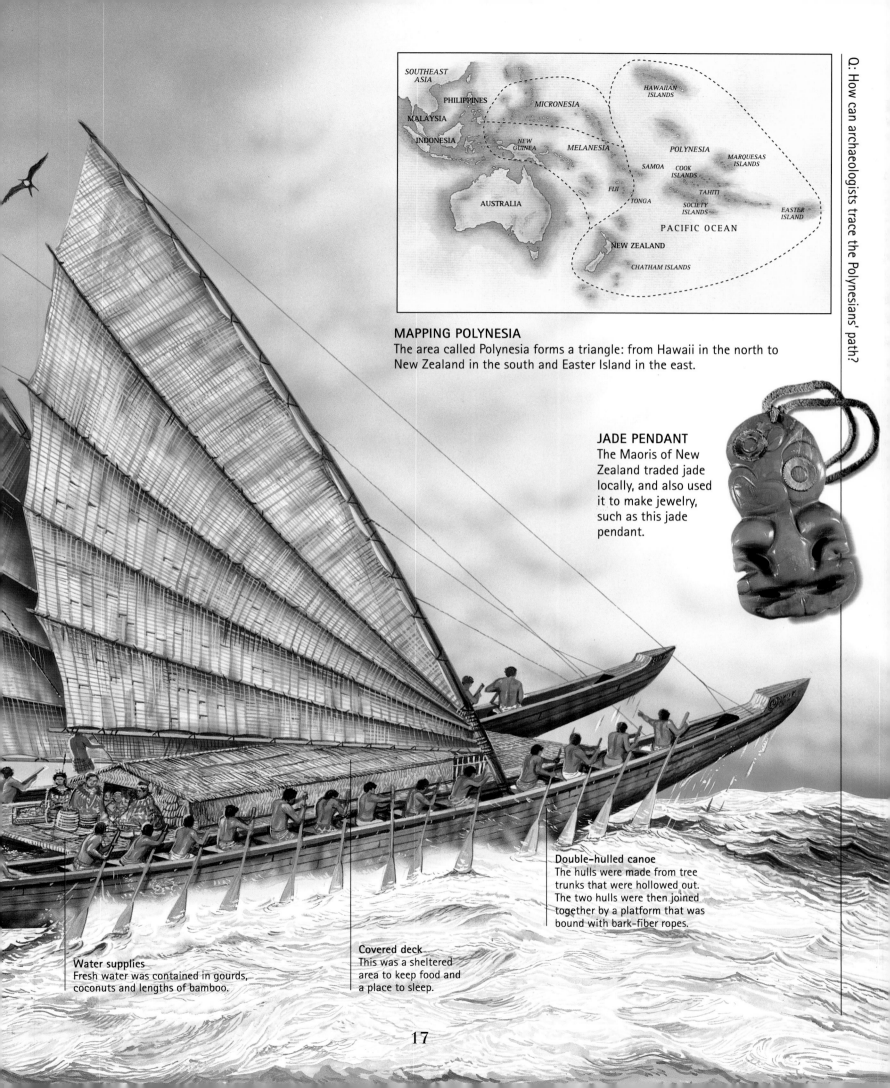

MAPPING POLYNESIA
The area called Polynesia forms a triangle: from Hawaii in the north to New Zealand in the south and Easter Island in the east.

JADE PENDANT
The Maoris of New Zealand traded jade locally, and also used it to make jewelry, such as this jade pendant.

Double-hulled canoe
The hulls were made from tree trunks that were hollowed out. The two hulls were then joined together by a platform that was bound with bark-fiber ropes.

Water supplies
Fresh water was contained in gourds, coconuts and lengths of bamboo.

Covered deck
This was a sheltered area to keep food and a place to sleep.

17

The Silk Road

A WINDING ROAD
Chinese traders make camp on their difficult and dangerous journey along the Silk Road. Often, they sold their goods to other merchants on the Silk Road, who then traveled to markets in the Middle East.

Trade routes began to link the civilizations of the ancient world. China had been isolated for centuries by mountains, forests and harsh deserts. The world beyond seemed hostile. Around 138 BC, the Chinese went outside these boundaries to look for allies against invading tribes from the north, and to find strong horses for their heavily armed warriors. They brought back news of other countries and exotic goods. Traders and travelers began to journey to and from China along a network of trade routes called the Silk Road, which crossed the whole continent of Asia. It became a highway for goods, ideas, knowledge, skills and religions. Camel caravans from China carrying silk and porcelain struggled through sandstorms in the Gobi Desert and across high mountains on the way through India and central Asia to the Middle East and Europe. The Silk Road also joined up with sea routes, and local traders filtered goods through to the Indian Ocean and the Mediterranean.

MONEY, MONEY
Ancient Chinese coins had holes in the middle so they could be carried on strings. This made it easy for Chinese traders to keep control of large sums of money.

WORSHIPPING BUDDHA
Chinese travelers brought Buddhism back from India. It is still an important religion in China.

ACROSS A CONTINENT
The Silk Road connected traders and travelers from different countries.

THE SECRET OF SILK
The Chinese were famous for their silk and they guarded carefully the secret of silk making. This delicate and precious fabric was woven from the fibers of the silkworm's cocoon (left). More than 2,500 cocoons must be unwound by hand to make just 7 oz (500 g) of yarn. The Chinese embroidered the silk cloth, painted it or made it into clothes. Many Chinese families bred silkworms so they could spin and weave their own silk. In this tenth-century Tang painting, the women of the royal court are pounding newly woven silk with wooden poles to soften it.

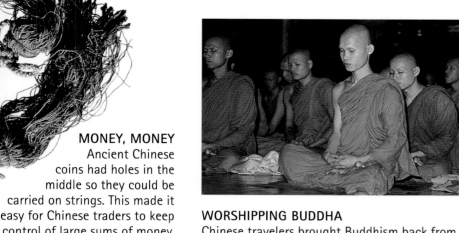

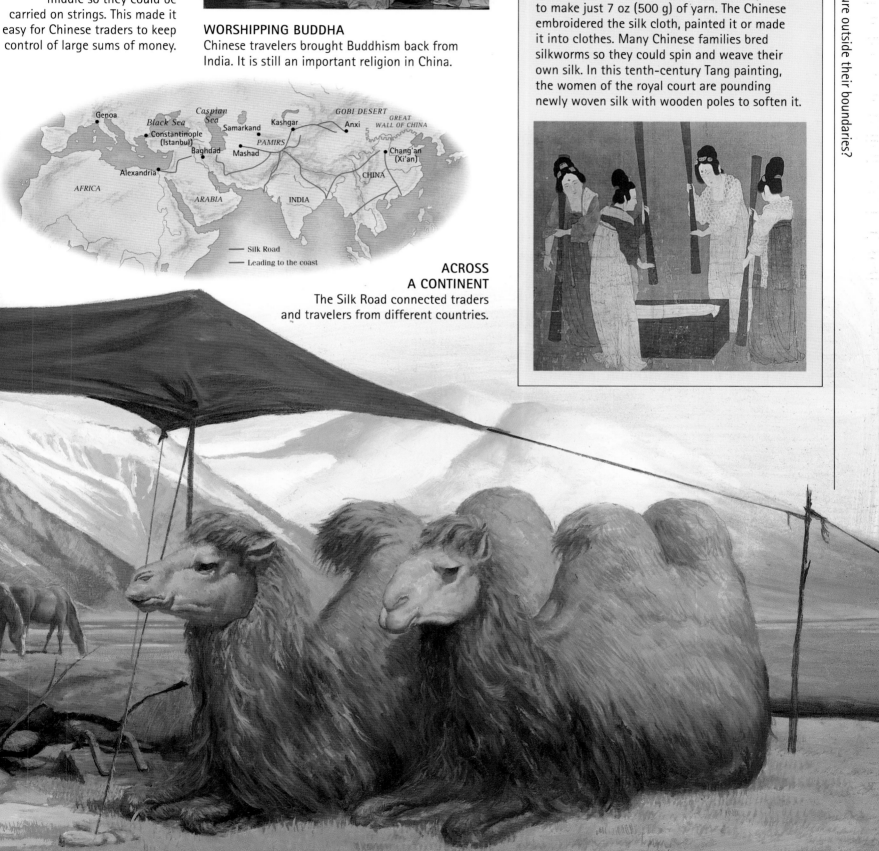

THE HOLY CITY
Christians, Muslims and Jews all believe that Jerusalem is a holy city. In the First Crusade, which was in 1099, Christian soldiers assembled at Constantinople (today's Istanbul) and marched to Jerusalem. They captured and ransacked the city, but it was eventually retaken by the Muslims.

PILGRIM'S FLASK
Pilgrims had traveled to the Holy Land for centuries. They made the long and difficult journey in the hope that God would forgive them their sins. They brought back reminders of their pilgrimages, such as holy water in flasks.

• TRAVEL AND TRADE •

The Crusades

In 1095, Pope Urban II called for a holy war, a crusade, to win the Holy Land (Palestine) from the Muslims. He promised a place in Heaven to all who took arms. During the next 200 years, kings and knights from Europe led three main crusades against the Muslims, who now blocked pilgrims from going to the land where Jesus Christ had lived and taught. There were also unofficial crusades, such as the People's Crusade in 1095, which was made up mainly of peasants. In 1212, more than 30,000 children set out for Palestine. Most never returned home. While many people fought and died in the battles for the Holy Land, others saw the crusades as a chance to trade and to make money. Ship owners in Venice, Pisa and Genoa, the Italian cities bordering the Mediterranean, took crusaders to the Holy Land. These cities became important trading centers where European goods were exchanged for those from the Middle East, Africa and Asia. The West learned much from the East during the crusades, such as ancient philosophy, techniques for weaving and making silk fabrics, and new architectural styles.

TRADING WITH THE EAST

Ship owners in Genoa, Pisa and Venice took the Christian armies across the Mediterranean. As a reward, they were given trading concessions in Muslim lands and cities, such as Constantinople, which had been conquered during the crusades. They now had direct access to the trade routes of Asia. The Italian cities grew wealthy from their trading links with the Muslims, but a bitter rivalry grew up between them and Constantinople. In 1204, the Venetians were chosen to lead the Fourth Crusade against Alexandria, but they attacked Constantinople instead.

LEAVING HOME
Men left their wives and children to join the crusades. They traveled great distances and fought in terrible battles. Many also died from diseases and lack of food.

LIVING IN THE EAST
The crusaders were impressed with the luxury, lifestyle and learning they found in the East. They enjoyed delicacies such as raisins, sugar and figs. In times of truce, some played games such as chess with the Saracens (Muslim fighters). They returned to Europe with a great desire for the riches of the East.

CROSSING THE DESERT
A camel caravan straggles across the Sahara Desert as it approaches an oasis town for supplies of food and water. Traders brought European goods, such as cloth and manufactured goods, into Africa by camel caravans. On the return journey, the camels carried gold, ivory and hides, while slaves walked slowly behind them in chains.

SALT FROM THE DESERT
Salt was very precious in ancient times. It was often traded gram for gram for gold. Most of the salt was produced in the Sahara. Water was poured into hollows in the soil (bottom left) and when the water dried in the sun, it left a small pile of salt. This was scooped out and packed into blocks as shown.

FROM HERE TO TIMBUKTU
From the 1200s to the 1500s, Timbuktu was one of the richest towns in Africa. Traders brought salt, cloth, copper, dates, figs and metal goods to Timbuktu where they traded for gold, ivory, cola nuts and slaves.

• TRAVEL AND TRADE •

Ships of the Desert

The Sahara is the largest desert in the world. A desolate expanse, it spreads for more than 3,490 miles (5,630 km) across North Africa. Traders crossed this bleak terrain with camels—their ships of the desert. These creatures could carry heavy loads and cover 20-25 miles (30-40 km) a day without food or water. Traders and their camel caravans brought goods from Europe and the Middle East into the heart of Africa, resting at scattered oases on the way. They also brought valuable salt, which was used to preserve meat. Salt was mined in the center of the Sahara but was very scarce in West African states, such as Ghana and Mali. The rulers of these lands paid for the salt and other goods with slaves and their plentiful supply of gold. The journey across the Sahara was always hazardous. Tuareg tribesmen in blue-veiled turbans sometimes attacked the caravans, and traders and camels could die in the blistering heat of the desert if the wells at the oases had dried up.

GUARDING THE GOLD
West Africa was very rich in gold, which was used to make coins. Soldiers such as this one guarded the gold when it was taken to trading posts in the Sahara.

23

European Trade

Europe began to prosper in the eleventh and twelfth centuries, during a period called the Middle Ages. Farming methods had improved and the population was increasing. Everyone had their place in this medieval society. The way of life was controlled by a system we call feudalism. Feudal society was made up of three groups: those who fought, such as kings, nobles and knights; those who worked, such as peasants; and those who prayed, such as the clergy. Land was handed down through the different groups—from the king to the peasant—in return for service, loyalty and protection. As trade grew, merchants became a powerful and wealthy new class outside the feudal society. Craftspeople also developed their skills. Some rulers, such as King Edward III (above left), taxed trade and tried to control it. The Italian cities of Genoa and Venice controlled the Mediterranean and trade with Asia, while German and northern European cities joined together to form the Hanseatic League. With a fleet of cargo ships called cogs, the League dominated trade in northern Europe until the end of the fifteenth century.

LOCAL TRADE
Towns, such as Champagne in France, were lively scenes of local trade. The narrow streets were lined with small shops. Often all the people in one trade or selling goods of one kind would work in the same street.

22

GUILD SEAL

Workers organized themselves into powerful groups called guilds, which set out rules for their members. They also set standards of quality for their work. Each guild had its own seal, such as this, which they used on all official documents.

ITALIAN BANKING

As trade grew in the 1200s, merchant companies with agents throughout the country found it dangerous to carry money between towns. Banks grew up in northern Italy as places where people could deposit money with a company in one town in return for a letter of credit. When they traveled to another town, they could draw the same sum from the company's agent there. Money soon became more important than land. Society began to change, and feudalism gradually collapsed.

DID YOU KNOW?

The bubonic plague, called the Black Death, ravaged Europe in the Middle Ages. The disease was carried by flea-infested rats that arrived in 1347 on a Genoese ship that had been trading in the Black Sea. It spread through towns and villages and killed about one-third of the population.

JOINING THE LEAGUE

A Hanseatic cog loads up with goods at Hamburg in Germany. The Hanseatic League was very powerful in the 1300s, and it controlled many of the markets of Europe. If a town refused to join the League, its merchants were not allowed to trade in these markets.

Discover more in Around the World

DID YOU KNOW?

The hump of a camel is actually a lump of fat. When food is hard to get in the desert, the camel gets energy from the fat. The hump shrinks as the camel uses the fat, but it grows again when the camel eats well for a few weeks.

A FAMOUS TRAVELER

Ibn Batuta, shown here meeting a Delhi sultan, was a famous Arab traveler. In 1325, he left his home in Tangier to make a pilgrimage to Mecca. He continued to travel for the next 24 years, visiting Persia, eastern Africa, central Asia, Siberia, India, Ceylon, Sumatra and China. He also crossed the Sahara to visit Timbuktu, capital of the ancient African kingdom of Mali. Ibn Batuta recorded everything he saw. People were then able to read about the customs and geography of many different countries.

MAPPING THE SAHARA

Donkeys, camels and people carried goods across different parts of the desert. This map shows the major trading posts and routes of the Sahara as well as the gold mines and oases.

Algiers
Tangier
Tunis
Mediterranean Sea
Tripoli
Sijilmasa
Alexandria
SAHARA DESERT
Zuilia
Asiut
Tuat
Ghat
Red Sea
River Nile
Ghiarou
Timbuktu
Niani
Manan
AFRICA
Axim
Elmina
Benin

■ Oases
▲ Gold mines
Camel caravans
Donkey caravans
Carried by people

Venice

Departure
In 1271, 17-year-old Marco Polo sailed from Venice with his father and uncle to the port of Acre in Palestine.

Constantinople (Istanbul)

OPENING UP ASIA
Genghis Khan united the nomadic Mongolian tribes and defeated the Turkish Muslims. He allowed European Christians to travel overland to the East.

Acre

The journey out
From Acre, they rode camels to the Persian port of Hormuz, where they saw beautiful patterned silk.

Baghdad

Samarkand

Kerman

Hormuz

• JOURNEYS OF DISCOVERY •

Traveling East

Marco Polo (left) is one of the most famous travelers in history. In 1271, he left Venice for the mysterious East with his father and uncle, who had made the journey once already. They sailed down the Persian Gulf, then traveled inland over the high mountains of Afghanistan. They crossed the perilous Gobi Desert, where night winds wailed like eerie voices. After three years, they reached the court of Kublai Khan, the Mongolian emperor of China and grandson of the great Genghis Khan. Kublai Khan ruled an enormous empire. He welcomed the strangers and asked Marco Polo to travel around his vast empire. Marco Polo saw magnificent cities with canal systems, precious jewels, skilled craftspeople and palaces decorated with gold and silver. When the Polos returned to Venice, Marco was captured by the Genoese who were at war with the Venetians. Marco told another prisoner, Rustichello, about his amazing adventures, and Rustichello published them in a book called *The Description of the World*. Many did not believe Marco Polo's tales, but others dreamed of seeing the lands he described.

Close to home
The Polos left the princess here and traveled overland and then by sea to Venice.

——— Traveling to the East
——— Returning to Venice
——— Travels in China
——— Mongolian Empire

BY LAND AND BY SEA
The Polos traveled overland to the East, but returned by sea 24 years later. They saw lands and riches unknown to Europeans. Marco Polo recorded his observations of the people and the places. Tales of China and India inspired poets and explorers for years.

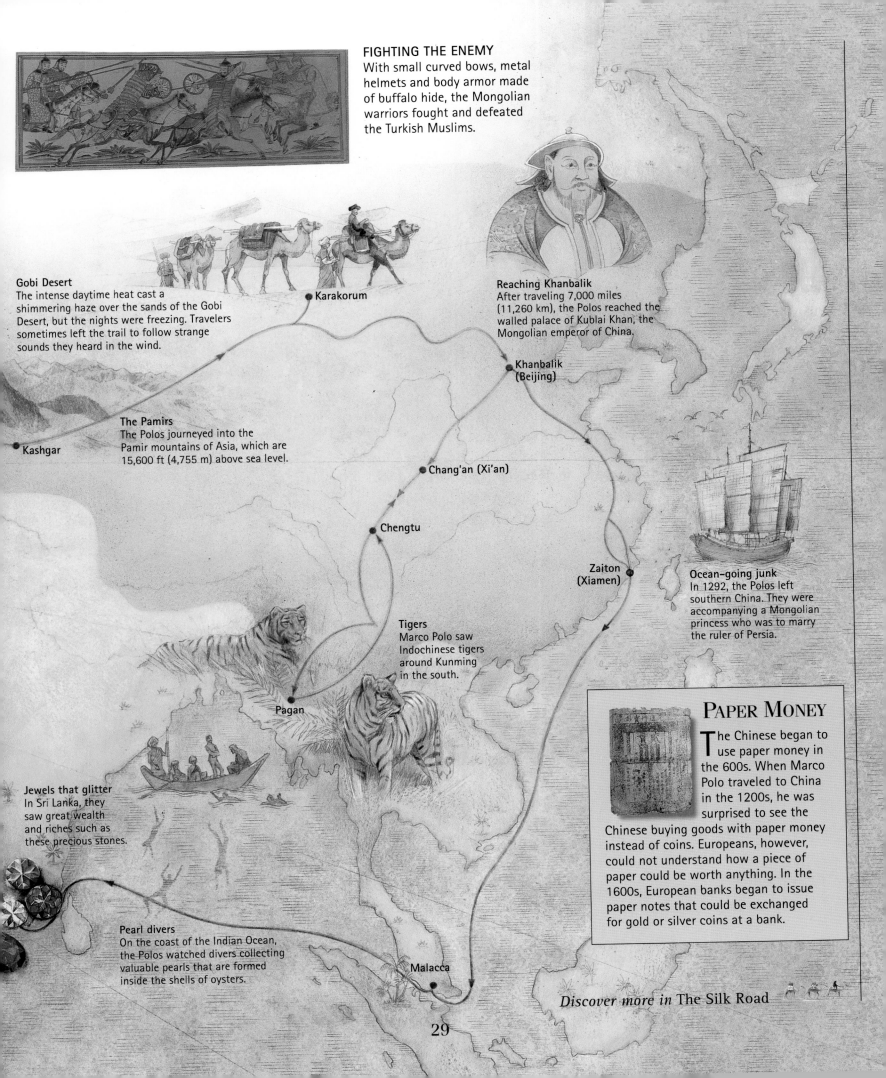

FIGHTING THE ENEMY
With small curved bows, metal helmets and body armor made of buffalo hide, the Mongolian warriors fought and defeated the Turkish Muslims.

Gobi Desert
The intense daytime heat cast a shimmering haze over the sands of the Gobi Desert, but the nights were freezing. Travelers sometimes left the trail to follow strange sounds they heard in the wind.

Karakorum

Reaching Khanbalik
After traveling 7,000 miles (11,260 km), the Polos reached the walled palace of Kublai Khan, the Mongolian emperor of China.

Khanbalik
(Beijing)

The Pamirs
The Polos journeyed into the Pamir mountains of Asia, which are 15,600 ft (4,755 m) above sea level.

Kashgar

Chang'an (Xi'an)

Chengtu

Zaiton
(Xiamen)

Ocean-going junk
In 1292, the Polos left southern China. They were accompanying a Mongolian princess who was to marry the ruler of Persia.

Tigers
Marco Polo saw Indochinese tigers around Kunming in the south.

Pagan

Jewels that glitter
In Sri Lanka, they saw great wealth and riches such as these precious stones.

PAPER MONEY

The Chinese began to use paper money in the 600s. When Marco Polo traveled to China in the 1200s, he was surprised to see the Chinese buying goods with paper money instead of coins. Europeans, however, could not understand how a piece of paper could be worth anything. In the 1600s, European banks began to issue paper notes that could be exchanged for gold or silver coins at a bank.

Pearl divers
On the coast of the Indian Ocean, the Polos watched divers collecting valuable pearls that are formed inside the shells of oysters.

Malacca

Discover more in The Silk Road

29

China Ventures Out

The Chinese rarely explored beyond their sea borders. While other nations set out on voyages to trade, to spread their religion, or to find new lands to settle, the Chinese felt they had all they needed in their own country. They did, however, want to show the rest of the world the power and strength of their empire. In the early 1400s, Ch'eng Tsu, the Emperor of the Ming dynasty, placed Admiral Zheng He in charge of a massive fleet of ocean-going junks. With 255 vessels, 62 enormous ships laden with treasure, and 28,000 men, Zheng He sailed grandly out of Nanking harbor, bound for the southern seas. Between 1405 and 1433, he led seven voyages, and his ships sailed to Southeast Asia, India, the Persian Gulf and Africa. Zheng He gave gifts of tea, silk and porcelain to the people he encountered on his travels. He returned to the Chinese court with foreign diplomats and exotic animals, such as giraffes.

FINDING THEIR WAY
Some of the greatest inventions come from China. Early sea compasses, such as this magnetized needle floating in a bowl of water, allowed sailors to navigate accurately across wide expanses of ocean.

SHIPS OF THE SEAS
Zheng He's junks were five times bigger than Portuguese caravels. Prince Henry of Portugal used some of the design features of the Chinese junk in his ships.

MAPPING ZHENG HE'S VOYAGES
Zheng He's seven voyages introduced many countries to the wealth and splendor of China.

DID YOU KNOW?
Zheng He's ships reached Africa in 1415 and rounded the Cape of Good Hope 70 years before the first Europeans. When Zheng He's voyages were over, the Chinese isolated themselves once more from the rest of the world.

GIFTS FOR THE EMPEROR
In 1414, Zheng He brought back ambassadors from east Africa and unusual presents. Here an attendant shows Ch'eng Tsu one of the gifts—a giraffe.

CHINESE PORCELAIN
Delicate Chinese porcelain was finer than any other pottery in the world. Made from a mixture of clays found only in China, it was highly prized and admired throughout the world. Traders brought Chinese porcelain to Europe in the twelfth century. It was so rare and expensive that only wealthy people could afford to buy it. European manufacturers tried to make porcelain themselves, but for a long time their porcelain could not compete with the high quality of Chinese porcelain.

Discover more in China and Japan Open Up

Passage to India

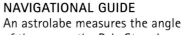

In the 1400s, the Portuguese led the race to find a sea route to the East. Prince Henry of Portugal ("the Navigator") set up a school of navigation, and explorers sailed along the west coast of Africa in small ships called caravels. At first, they did not sail far. They imagined that monsters and boiling seas awaited them in the hot lands to the south. In 1485, Diogo Cão reached Cape Cross and set up a stone marker called a *padrão*. Two years later, Bartolomeu Dias passed Cão's marker. He rounded the Cape of Good Hope and sailed into the Indian Ocean, but his fearful crew begged him to turn back. The explorer Vasco da Gama traded for gold, ivory and slaves in Africa and reached the Indian port of Calicut in 1498. He wanted to trade with the Indian princes, but they were unimpressed with the goods he offered them. So the Portuguese came with men and guns and used force to set up trading bases in India and Africa. Portugal soon became a powerful empire.

NAVIGATIONAL GUIDE
An astrolabe measures the angle of the sun or the Pole Star above the horizon. Sailors could tell from this reading how far south or north they had traveled.

VALUABLE IVORY
This African salt cellar, showing armed Portuguese on horses, was carved from ivory. The Africans traded ivory with the Portuguese.

LOOKING EAST
Prince Henry never went on a sea voyage himself, but he still inspired many great Portuguese explorers.

SAILING TO THE EAST
The Portuguese ships stayed close to the coast and followed familiar landmarks as they sailed to Africa. The Portuguese were welcomed in some lands, but mistrusted in others. They often overpowered the local people with guns.

PTOLEMY'S WORLD
The Greek astronomer and mathematician Ptolemy drew this map in AD 150. It shows only the top half of Africa because no-one knew how far south it spread. The first Portuguese explorers also thought the world looked like this.

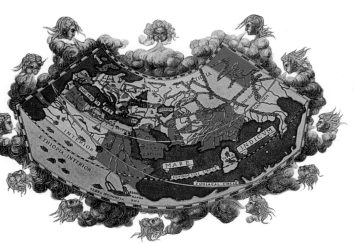

SPICES FOR SALE

Spices were precious in the 1400s. People did not have refrigerators, so spices disguised the taste of old meat. Pepper was so rare that it was sometimes used instead of money. The Portuguese discovered that most of the spices sold in India did not come from there. Cloves, mace and nutmeg, the most valuable spices, came from the Molucca Islands further to the east. They became known as the Spice Islands.

SAILING TO GLORY
Blessed by King Manuel I and officials from the church, Vasco da Gama left Lisbon in 1498, bound for India. His four ships were stocked with enough supplies for three years. They battled storms and unpredictable currents, and many sailors died from scurvy.

Sailing West

The Italian explorer Christopher Columbus (left) believed he would reach the East if he sailed west. Like many others, Columbus had no idea that the Americas, discovered by the Vikings many hundreds of years before, even existed. He imagined that most of the world was covered by one huge piece of land, made up of Europe, Africa and Asia. Columbus persuaded King Ferdinand and Queen Isabella of Spain to finance a sea voyage. In 1492, he sailed from Spain with his ships the *Niña*, the *Pinta* and the *Santa Maria*. When Columbus saw the Caribbean islands, he thought they were the islands near mainland Asia and he called them the West Indies. He found strange new foods and animals, which he took back to the Spanish court. Columbus made three more voyages across the Atlantic, and explored many of the Caribbean islands and parts of the Central American coast. He always believed he had discovered Asia, but others soon suspected he had found a "New World."

DID YOU KNOW?

The people of the West Indies slept in hanging beds called "harmorcas." Columbus's sailors copied this idea and made these beds above the dirty, wet decks, away from the scurrying rats. They called their beds hammocks.

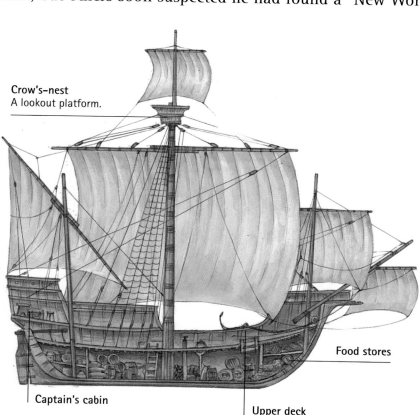

Crow's-nest
A lookout platform.

Food stores

Captain's cabin

Upper deck
The sailors slept here and prepared their meals.

A MODEL FLAGSHIP

The *Santa Maria* was Columbus's flagship. No-one knows what it really looked like, but models have been built that give us some idea. The *Santa Maria* was slower and heavier than the other two ships. It was wrecked off the island of Hispaniola (now Haiti) in 1492.

A MEETING OF WORLDS

Columbus landed on San Salvador in the Bahamas and claimed it for Spain. The people on the island were friendly toward the strangers.

LAND AHOY!

After more than a month at sea, Columbus's crew were weary and disgruntled. They wanted to turn back. But a cry from the crow's-nest soon lifted their spirits. Land was in sight!

BETWEEN TWO WORLDS

Columbus did not find Asia, but he did link the Eastern and Western hemispheres—the Old and the New worlds. Soon, food and animals began to pass between them. The Europeans brought horses, sheep, pigs, wheat, sugar cane, wheeled transport, iron and steel to the New World. They returned to Europe with potatoes, pineapples, avocados, tomatoes, corn, kidney beans, vanilla, peanuts, turkeys, cocoa, tobacco and rubber.

Discover more in The Vikings

Spain and the New World

Spanish conquistadors (conquerors) set sail for the New World early in the sixteenth century. Lured by thoughts of gold and power, they followed Columbus's route across the Atlantic in sturdy galleons. Catholic priests accompanied them to convert the peoples of the new lands to Christianity. The New World was all they had hoped it would be. The Aztecs of Mexico and the Incas of Peru were highly organized societies that had existed for hundreds of years. The Spanish conquistadors were dazzled by the gold and silver treasures and the magnificent stone cities, pyramids, temples and sculptures, which were built by the people without iron tools or the wheel. In 1521, Hernando Cortés captured Tenochtitlán, the Aztec capital. Francisco Pizarro reached the center of the Inca Empire in the Andes Mountains in 1532. On horseback and armed with guns, the Spaniards defeated the large numbers of Aztecs and Incas. They soon controlled this rich new world.

ISLAND CAPITAL
Tenochtitlán, the spectacular Aztec capital, was built on an island in a lake. It was destroyed by the Spanish conquistador Hernando Cortés in 1521, but was later rebuilt as Mexico City.

BEADS OF PRAYER
The Catholic priests who traveled to the New World wore rosary beads. These help people to concentrate when they are praying and to remember how many prayers they have said.

DID YOU KNOW?
The Europeans brought many infectious diseases, such as measles, smallpox and even colds, to the New World. The people there had no resistance to such diseases, and many died. Their traditions and customs died with them.

TREASURES OF GOLD
The Spanish conquistadors found great treasures in the New World. The Incas used this gold figure, made in the shape of a winged god, in religious ceremonies.

THE TREATY OF TORDESILLAS

As Portugal and Spain began to expand their empires, they argued over who should own the new lands. In 1494, Pope Alexander VI arranged a treaty to prevent any disputes. He drew a line down the map of the world (above). Any land that was discovered east of this line belonged to Portugal, while land found to the west belonged to Spain. Although Brazil is in South America, it was claimed by Portugal when it was discovered because it fell east of the line. France, England and Holland were angered by this treaty because it meant they could not share in the riches of the New World.

SAILING THE OCEAN BLUE

Galleons filled with gold and silver from Mexico and Peru sailed across the Atlantic Ocean. Much of the gold mined by the Spaniards in South America was made into coins. The riches of the New World made the kings of Spain very powerful. They often sent armed ships to protect the galleons from pirates.

STORMY STRAIT
Magellan had discovered a passage to the East, but rowboats had to guide his ships through the rough waters. When Magellan emerged into a calm ocean on the other side, he named it the Pacific—the peaceful sea.

PEARLS FOR THE QUEEN
Queen Elizabeth I of England encouraged Francis Drake to loot Spanish ships on his voyages. She gave him money and ships and shared in the treasure he brought back. Here, Drake presents the Queen with a pearl necklace on board his ship the *Golden Hind*.

• THE NEW WORLD •

Around the World

As ships began to sail in all directions across the oceans, knowledge of the world grew. Like Columbus, the Portuguese explorer Ferdinand Magellan (left) believed that he could find a westward route to the Spice Islands. He persuaded Charles I of Spain to sponsor his voyage. Magellan set out across the Atlantic in 1519 with five ships. He discovered the treacherous and stormy passage at the bottom of South America, now called the Strait of Magellan. In 1521, he arrived at the Philippine islands. He had reached the East by sailing west. Magellan was killed in the Philippines, but his crew on the ship *Victoria* sailed on to Spain. Fifty-six years later, the brilliant English navigator Francis Drake set out to explore the southern seas and sail around the world. He journeyed up the west coast of South America, raiding Spanish ports and seizing the cargo of Spanish ships. The Spaniards were furious! Relations between Spain and England deteriorated and in 1588 Philip II sent the Spanish Armada to invade England. His warships, however, were unsuccessful.

DRAKE'S TRAVELS
In 1577, Drake sailed from Plymouth, England, on his most famous voyage. Three years later he returned a hero. He had circumnavigated the world.

THE MANILA GALLEONS

Ferdinand Magellan claimed the Philippines for Spain in 1521. About 50 years later, Spanish galleons began to sail from Acapulco (today's Mexico) across the Pacific to the port of Manila in the Philippines. Manila became a trading center for India, Southeast Asia, Japan and China. Galleons carried European products and Mexican silver to Manila and returned to Spain loaded with riches from the East. Some galleons, such as the *Nuestra Señora de la Concepción*, were shipwrecked on the perilous route. Its cargo of jewels, silks, spices and porcelain sank with the ship to the ocean floor.

Breaking the Ice

In the 1500s, Spain and Portugal controlled the southern routes to the East. Other countries were forced to seek another way to sail from the Atlantic to the Pacific—a northwest passage. In 1497, Italian John Cabot followed the routes of fishermen who caught cod in the cold North Atlantic Ocean and discovered Newfoundland. Frenchman Jacques Cartier found the St. Lawrence River, which became the main route into northern North America, and fur traders soon moved into the area. In 1576, Englishman Martin Frobisher explored Canada's northeast coast and reached Baffin Island. Another Englishman, Henry Hudson, named the Hudson River, the Hudson Strait and Hudson Bay. But these explorers did not have suitable clothes or ships to survive the winter in this vast area of islands and rivers, and they did not discover a northwest passage. Sir John Franklin found this ice-bound route when he explored the Arctic between 1845 and 1848, but no-one sailed through it until 1906.

IN THE NAME OF THE KING
In the service of Henry VII of England, John Cabot sailed west from Bristol to find a route to the Spice Islands. He opened up Canada to the world.

DANGEROUS JOURNEYS
The cold northern seas challenged explorers. Even when the water seemed calm, long winters and a landscape of ice made their journeys difficult and slow. Ships often became trapped in ice for months. Many men suffered from scurvy and died in the terrible conditions.

WALRUS IVORY
The Inuit (Eskimos) lived on the northern coast of Canada as well as in Alaska and Siberia. They traded in furs and ivory.

CAST ADRIFT

Henry Hudson made three journeys to the northern seas. During the bitter winter of 1610, Hudson's crew mutinied when he wanted to continue the voyage north. The mutineers put Hudson, his son and loyal crew members in a boat without oars, water or fresh food. They were never seen again.

GREENLAND

ICELAND

BAFFIN
ISLAND

Hudson
Bay

NORTH
ATLANTIC
OCEAN

ENGLAND

NORTH
AMERICA

NEWFOUNDLAND

FRANCE

Great
Lakes

— Cabot 1497
— Cartier 1535-6
— Frobisher 1576
— Hudson 1610

EXPLORING NORTH AMERICA

Many places in the north of Canada are named after the explorers who died trying to find a northwest passage.

HUDSON BAY TRADING POST

In 1670, a group of wealthy English merchants and noblemen set up the Hudson's Bay Company. King Charles II of England said the company could trade in all the lands drained by the streams that flowed into Hudson Bay. Trading posts and forts were built all along the bay. The Inuit (Eskimos) traded the skins and furs of wild animals with the Europeans for arms and other goods.

Discover more in Russian Trade

A PIRATE'S PISTOL
A pirate carried several weapons, such as a dagger, an axe, a curved sword called a cutlass and a pistol.

Pirates

Pirates had roamed the seas for centuries, attacking ships and stealing their cargoes. In the 1500s, however, the pickings were especially rich. Spanish galleons filled with gold, silver and emeralds from the New World crossed the Atlantic. Ships laden with spices and silks sailed along the trade routes in the Mediterranean and the Indian Ocean. Because England, France and Holland were often at war with Spain, their rulers gave sailors called "privateers" permission to attack Spanish ships and steal their treasures for the government. When peace was made with Spain in the 1600s, many privateers became pirates. They set up bases in the West Indies and Madagascar and attacked ships from every country. The life of a pirate appealed to poorly paid, harshly treated sailors. Henry Morgan was the most successful pirate in the 1650s, while "Blackbeard" Edward Teach terrorized the American East Coast in the 1700s.

DID YOU KNOW?
Pirate flags fluttered menacingly in the wind as pirate ships sailed the seas. At first, pirate captains had their own flags, such as this one. In the 1700s, the Jolly Roger became the common pirate flag.

SHIPMATES, TO ARMS!
Using hooks and ropes to keep the ships together, pirates scramble on board a Spanish trading ship. The crew fight fiercely on deck, but the pirates outnumber them. Pirates often gave defeated crews a choice: join them or die!

SMUGGLERS' COVE
As trading ships began to sail in all directions around the world, trade became more organized. Many governments demanded that traders pay special taxes on goods they brought into the country. They placed agents at sea ports to make sure this money was paid. Smugglers avoided paying the tax by bringing goods into the country secretly. They sailed their ships into deserted coves away from the main ports, and rowed ashore in the black of night to unload their cargoes.

PORTRAIT OF A PIRATE
A pirate robbed ships for himself and was hanged if he was caught. A privateer, however, had a special document from his government that made it legal for him to capture the ships of an enemy.

43

The Dutch Influence

E very country in Europe wanted a share of the East and its riches. The Spaniards and Portuguese dominated trade with the East in the 1500s, but the Dutch, English and French soon began to challenge them. In 1602, the Dutch government formed the Dutch East India Company, which based itself in Batavia, on the island of Java in the East Indies (now Indonesia). This company bypassed the main spice-trade ports in the Indian Ocean and China, which were controlled by the Portuguese. The English also formed their own East India Company and became a great rival of the Dutch. The Dutch, however, were the strongest in the seventeenth century. Between 1618 and 1629, they even drove the Portuguese out of the prized Spice Islands. The Dutch created a vast trading network in the East Indies. They encouraged the islanders to grow new crops such as tea, coffee, sugar and tobacco. Eager to develop other trade links, the Governor of the Dutch East Indies sent Abel Tasman to the South Pacific in 1642. He visited New Zealand, and in 1644 he explored the northern and western coasts of Australia. But the Dutch were unimpressed with the trade opportunities in these distant lands and did not explore them further.

EAST INDIAMEN
The heavily armed Dutch merchant ships were called East Indiamen. They carried cargoes of gold from the Netherlands to India and the Far East, where they loaded up with spices, tea, jade, porcelain and jewelry for the markets in Europe.

DELFTWARE
Dutch art and crafts flourished in the 1600s. Craftspeople in the town of Delft made a distinctive blue and white earthenware of the same name. It was shipped abroad and bought by the wealthy.

NORTH AMERICA
The Dutch also looked west for trading opportunities. In 1612, Dutch explorers settled on an island in the Hudson River, which they called New Amsterdam. The English captured it in 1664 and renamed it New York. This map shows the English fleet in the harbor.

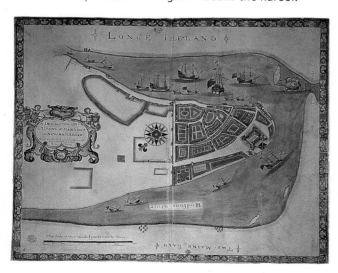

PICKING THE COFFEE BERRIES
Javanese women carry baskets of coffee berries on their heads. Coffee comes from red berries that grow on shrubs. Each berry contains two beans, which are roasted and processed. By 1720, the Dutch were the largest suppliers of coffee to Europe, where coffee houses were very popular.

DUTCH EAST INDIA COMPANY

The Dutch East India Company was very powerful. For nearly 200 years, the Dutch traded between Asia and the Netherlands and ruled the islands of present-day Indonesia. They had well-positioned bases along their trade routes, and offices abroad, such as this one in London. By 1700, the company controlled the cinnamon, clove and nutmeg trade in the East Indies. They also established a trading base and settlement in South Africa.

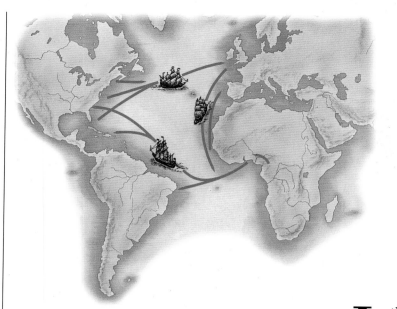

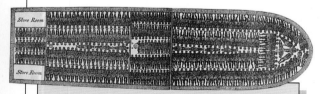

A TRIANGLE OF TRADE
Traders loaded their ships in European ports, then sailed to Africa, where they bought slaves. They sold the slaves in the New World. The goods they bought there became the return cargo to Europe.

DID YOU KNOW?
Slaves were crammed side by side on shelves or platforms inside the holds of the ships for up to two months. Amid the filthy conditions on board, diseases spread rapidly. Many slaves died during the voyage to the New World.

• THE BUSINESS OF TRADE •
Slave Trade

In the 1500s, traders from many countries began to buy and sell Africans to work in the New World. The Spaniards there needed workers for their gold and silver mines, because many Native Americans had been killed during the Spanish conquests or had died from European diseases. So the Spaniards looked to Africa. Slave hunters raided inland villages and captured men, women and children. They were taken to the coast where the Europeans bought them from local African chiefs for goods such as guns and copper. The slaves were bound in chains, shipped across the Atlantic and sold at the New World ports. Later, slaves were also sold to European settlers in the West Indies and North America to work on the sugar, tobacco and cotton plantations. The slaves were branded by their new owners and taken to the fields or mines, where they worked from sunrise to sunset. In the 1700s, several million Africans were sent to the New World. Europe and the New World became rich from the slave trade, but Africa lost many of its people and traditions.

SHACKLES
The slaves were shackled in chains such as these during the long voyage across the Atlantic to stop them from jumping overboard.

WORKING IN THE FIELD
Slaves on a Caribbean sugar plantation harvest the crop, pick up the trimmed sugar cane and tie it in bundles.

MAKING SUGAR
The slaves carried the bundles to the crushing machine, which forced a sweet juice from the stalks. This cane juice was used to make sugar, rum and molasses. The owners of the plantations lived in great style and bought more slaves with their profits.

46

AGAINST SLAVERY

THE LIBERATOR.

The slave trade thrived in the 1700s, but many people were against it. They said that slavery took away the basic right of all humans to be free. William Wilberforce led a movement to stop slavery in the British Empire. When slavery was outlawed there in 1807, he began to campaign against the foreign slave trade. *The Liberator* was an anti-slavery journal published in Boston by William Lloyd Garrison. By the end of the 1800s, most nations had abolished slavery.

Russian Trade

In the 1500s, Russia began to extend its borders. Russian tsars conquered neighboring lands and sent peasant soldiers, called Cossacks, to explore parts of Siberia—a cold, harsh land to the east with many raw materials. The English and Dutch, searching for a northeast passage to the Spice Islands, began to trade with Russia for furs. In 1672, Peter the Great became Tsar of Russia. He was determined to make his country a world power. He traveled to western European countries to study their societies and economies, and their shipbuilding techniques. He expanded Russia's territory to the Baltic Sea and in 1703 founded St. Petersburg to give Russia a port that was close to the west. Because the Russians did not know how far to the east their vast country stretched, Peter the Great hired Danish explorer Vitus Bering. In 1728, Bering sailed between Russia and Alaska and discovered the Northeast Passage. Russian hunters trapped fur seals, sea otters and walruses along the Alaskan coast, and the fur trade flourished.

LIVING ON THE EDGE
The ancestors of this 1890s Cossack were peasant soldiers who lived in the frontier areas of the Russian Empire. They fought for the tsars and were given many privileges. They were the first people to open up Siberia in the east.

FROM THE NORTH POLE
The Russians increased their trade outlets by establishing St. Petersburg and opening up the Northeast Passage from the top of Scandinavia to the Bering Sea.

CAPITAL BY THE SEA

St. Petersburg became the capital of Russia in 1712. This beautiful city was an important center for trade with the west.

NORTHEAST PASSAGE

Baron Nils A. E. Nordenskjöld was a Swedish polar explorer. In 1879, he became the first person to sail through the Northeast Passage that connected the Atlantic and Pacific oceans. He tells of the journey in his book, *Voyage of the Vega.*

EXCHANGE OF GOODS

Russian fur trappers from northwest Russia show their polar fox pelts to English traders from the Muscovy Company. The traders would anchor in a White Sea bay and row ashore to meet the trappers. The English exchanged woolen cloth for furs.

BREAKING THROUGH

The Northeast Passage is bitterly cold and frozen with ice. Icebreakers are specially designed, powerful ships that can forge a path through ice. They force their bows up onto the top of the ice until the weight of the ship makes the ice collapse. Since the 1930s, Russian ships have sailed regularly through the Northeast Passage to the Bering Sea, opening up new trade routes.

Discover more in Breaking the Ice

CHURCH AT GOA
The Portuguese made Goa their capital in India. They built churches such as this to try to convert the local people to Christianity.

India's Wealth

India seemed a place of great wealth to the Europeans. The ruling Mogul emperors had magnificent palaces and treasures, and the country was rich in gold, jewels, spices and cotton. Vasco da Gama led the Portuguese to India in 1498 and they traded for spices and luxury goods from their coastal base at Goa. London merchants formed the British East India Company in 1600 and made Bombay their headquarters, while the French arrived in India in 1668. When the rule of the Mogul emperors weakened in the middle of the 1700s, the French and British began to fight each other for control of India. The British eventually won, and by the early nineteenth century all Indian states were under British rule. Queen Victoria took the title "Empress of India" in 1877. The British now had unlimited access to the wealth of India. They sent goods and raw materials back to England, where the Industrial Revolution had created radical changes in the way goods were produced and transported. Trade was entering a new stage.

GRACEFUL CLIPPER
Clippers with billowing canvas sails carried goods from India and China on most trade routes until faster steamers took over in the 1860s.

TEA FOR TWO
An official from the British East India Company drinks tea with an Indian prince. Before the British arrived, Indian princes ruled most of India. By the nineteenth century, however, the British East India Company and the British government controlled the country. Many Englishmen made fortunes in India and they lived in great luxury.

INDIAN COTTON

People in India have grown cotton and woven its fibers by hand into cloth for thousands of years. At first, the English bought cloth from India, but then they began to import the raw cotton and weave it themselves by hand. As the demand for cloth became greater, machines were invented to weave large quantities of it. England became one of the largest producers of cloth in the world during the Industrial Revolution.

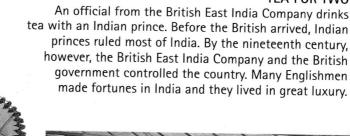

CURIOUS CREATURES
Indian elephants and rare animals were transported from India all around the world. People flocked to zoological gardens, such as this one in London, to see these unusual creatures.

The Heart of Africa

For hundreds of years, Africa seemed very mysterious to the Europeans. Sailors navigated around the continent but few explorers ventured into the interior. They knew there were jungles, swamps, deserts and vast plains with wild animals. Explorers also died from tropical diseases, such as malaria and yellow fever. Part of West Africa became known as the "White Man's Grave." Because Africa was rich in ivory, gold and slaves, many European countries set up trading ports on the African coast. In 1652, the Dutch East India Company established a supply base for its ships in Cape Colony, South Africa. The Arabs shipped slaves from the east coast of Africa to the Middle East and India, while on the west coast, Europeans took millions of slaves to the sugar and cotton plantations of the New World. Many people were appalled by the slave trade. They formed anti-slavery societies and encouraged Christian missionaries to travel to Africa to try to stop it. Dr. David Livingstone, a Scottish missionary and explorer, journeyed into the heart of Africa in 1849. The records he kept enticed other Europeans to follow his path. When diamonds and gold were discovered in South Africa in the late 1800s, immigrants poured into the country and settled large areas.

DISCOVERING DIAMONDS
Diamond fields were found near Kimberley in South Africa in 1868. As tons of rock must be mined and crushed to find one small diamond, a great deal of money and labor were needed to extract large amounts of diamonds.

SLAVES FOR THE NEW WORLD
The slave trade to the New World was at its peak in the 1700s. African chiefs would capture men and women from enemy tribes and sell them to the Europeans at trading bases on the coast.

EXPLORING AFRICA

Dr. David Livingstone was a famous missionary and explorer. He spent years in Africa, mapping the land and searching for rivers that could be navigated by missionaries and traders (above). When Livingstone disappeared for a few years, Henry Morton Stanley (left), an English reporter from the *New York Herald*, went to Africa to find him. In 1871, Stanley found Livingstone by Lake Tanganyika and greeted him with the famous words, "Dr. Livingstone, I presume?"

THE DUTCH INFLUENCE
The Dutch (Boers) settled in South Africa as farmers. When British settlers came to their colony in the 1830s, the Boers trekked into the interior. They founded the Transvaal and the Orange Free State.

STRIKING IT RICH
Two gold-miners dig painstakingly by candlelight. Miners first found gold in patchy seams in the rock, as seen here. Later, they discovered it in surface deposits and then in deep underground deposits.

China and Japan Open Up

The Japanese were astonished at the sight of the strange foreigners who sailed into Edo Bay in their black ships. Cautiously, they approached the steamships in small craft. The British, Russians and French soon followed the Americans into Japan. By the 1860s, many foreign diplomats and traders were living in Japan.

DUTCH BOY
From the 1600s to the 1850s, the Japanese allowed the Dutch to trade from an island in Nagasaki harbor. Japanese artists included Dutch figures in their art.

By the early 1800s, Europeans had set up trading bases in most countries except China and Japan. The Chinese hated foreign "barbarians" and allowed only Dutch and Portuguese merchants to trade in certain areas. Europeans first ventured into Japan in the 1500s, bringing Christianity with them. But in the 1600s, the ruling Tokugawa shoguns expelled all Europeans, except the Dutch. For the next 200 years, Japan was closed to the rest of the world. In the 1800s, the western powers tried to open up China and Japan for trade. In 1839, Britain went to war with China. Three years later, the Chinese signed a treaty giving Hong Kong to the British and allowing them to trade in other ports. In 1853, four American warships, led by Commodore Perry, sailed into Edo Bay (now Tokyo Bay) in Japan. Perry carried a letter from his president to the Japanese emperor, requesting trade ports. Japan and the United States signed a treaty a year later. The Japanese began to build railways and factories and soon became a major industrial nation.

JUST LIKE THE WEST
After 1854, many Japanese, including the royal family, gave up their traditional costumes for western clothes. They wanted their people to be as modern as those in the West.

OPIUM WARS
The British East India Company began to bring the drug opium into China from India to trade for Chinese tea. But it was illegal to trade in opium, and wars broke out between the Chinese government and the British.

BOXER REBELLION

Some Chinese hated anything that was foreign. They formed a secret group called Yihequan (Righteous and Harmonious Fists), nicknamed the "Boxers." In 1900, they attacked foreign factories, railways, churches and schools, and besieged diplomats in Peking for 55 days. Many Chinese and foreigners were killed in this rebellion.

Canals Linking Oceans

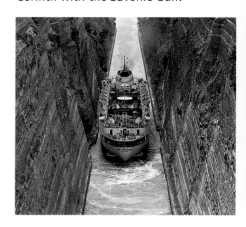

World trade flourished in the 1800s. Goods were produced quickly, cheaply and in great quantities during the Industrial Revolution. But merchant ships still had to carry their cargoes enormous distances around the world. In 1859, Frenchman Ferdinand de Lesseps began to build the Suez Canal to link the Mediterranean and the Red seas. It made the route between the United Kingdom and India 6,000 miles (9,700 km) shorter, and the world seemed much smaller. The Panama Canal, which links the Atlantic and Pacific oceans, was opened in 1914. Ferdinand Magellan and those who followed him had to sail around South America to reach the Pacific Ocean, but now ships could save 7,900 miles (12,600 km) by cutting through Central America. The Panama Canal was a great engineering achievement. For ten years, thousands of laborers cut through jungles, hills and swamps (above left), many suffering from tropical diseases. It is now the busiest canal in the world.

OPENING THE WAY
The 118-mile (190-km) long Suez Canal was opened by Empress Eugenie of France in 1869. Spectators lined the banks and steam boats formed a grand procession through the canal that would alter travel and trade across the world forever.

BIGGER AND BETTER

The Suez Canal has been widened several times to handle bigger ships and more traffic. Today, it is 36 ft (11 m) deeper than when it was first built, 230 ft (70 m) wider at the bottom and 512 ft (156 m) wider at the surface.

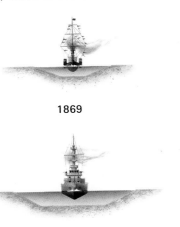

1869

1939

Today

LOCKED IN

Canals can be built across land that is not level. These canals have water-filled chambers, called locks, which separate two sections that are at different heights. To pass from one level to a higher level (right), a boat enters the lock. The gates close and water from the higher level flows in to raise the boat to that level. When the gates at the higher end are opened, the boat moves forward. To lower a boat, water from the lock flows out. Vessels traveling along the Panama Canal use the Gatún Locks (above left).

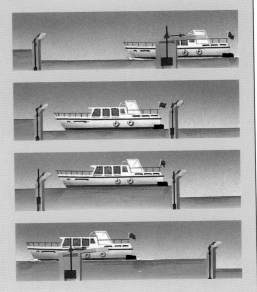

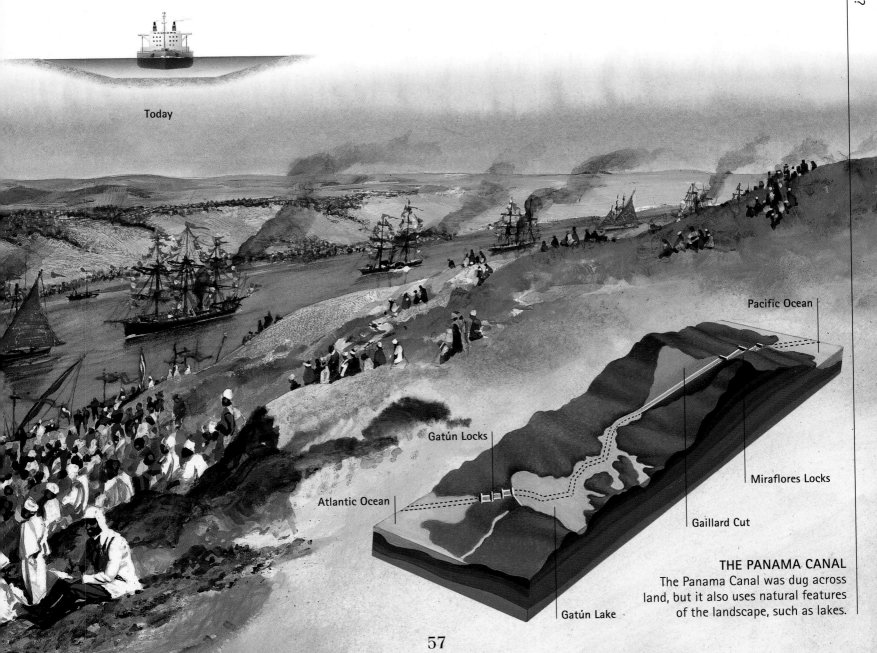

Pacific Ocean

Gatún Locks

Atlantic Ocean

Miraflores Locks

Gaillard Cut

Gatún Lake

THE PANAMA CANAL

The Panama Canal was dug across land, but it also uses natural features of the landscape, such as lakes.

Changes in Transportation

Trade is not possible without transportation. At first, our ancestors could trade only what they could carry. Then with pack animals, sleds and wheeled carts, they began to transport heavier goods. Eventually, sailing ships carried them beyond their shores, extending their world. Ideas, religions, skills, knowledge and goods passed between different peoples. Towns and cities grew, and civilization spread. At the end of the 1400s, ships became bigger and faster and navigation improved. The first engine-powered vehicles were invented in the early 1800s, and transportation has changed rapidly ever since. Steam engines powered trains and ships, and goods were carried in greater quantities. As traveling times became shorter, new items, such as fresh fruit and flowers, were transported across the world. In industrial countries today, goods are loaded onto trains, trucks, airplanes and ships. Jet airliners take travelers to destinations all around the world, while millions of people travel in cars and buses every day. Changes in transportation have revolutionized the way we trade and travel.

ON THE ROAD
Huge semi-trailers carry large amounts of cargo over long distances. Roads have to be very strong and well maintained to cope with such heavy vehicles.

LOADING UP
Cargo is loaded into the nose of a 747 freighter. Because there is limited space for cargo on airplanes, it is the most expensive way to send goods.

DID YOU KNOW?
Ice is one of the oldest ways to keep food fresh. The Chinese used it as long ago as 1000 BC. Technology has now made it possible to carry fresh foods long distances in refrigerated trucks, railway cars and the compartments of ships.

SHIPPING CARGO
The cheapest way to move general cargo is by water. Cargo ships travel mainly across oceans and on bodies of water linked to oceans, such as the Mediterranean Sea and the Baltic Sea.

SEEING THE WORLD

Traveling is an ancient pastime. The Arab traveler Ibn Batuta spent 24 years moving from country to country, while Marco Polo was one of the first Europeans to travel through the East. Today, transportation has made the world accessible to travelers. Tourists travel across the globe to see glimpses of the ancient world, such as the temple of Ramses II in Egypt (above).

CROSSING CONTINENTS
This 2-mile (3.8-km) long train stretches across the landscape in Western Australia. Its cargo of iron ore is being taken to the coast to be shipped to Japan. Freight is often carried by more than one form of transportation on the way to its final destination.

Shipping News

Egyptian trading boat
3000 BC to 500 BC.
Propelled by oars and sail.
Traders navigated by the stars,
currents, clouds, birds, fish
and mammals' movements.

Phoenician trading boat
1000 BC to 300 BC.
Hull covered with copper
for extra strength.

Viking knorr
AD 800 to AD 1070.
Overlapping planks
strengthened the hull.
Steered by single stern oar.

Polynesian canoe
Early AD onward.
Two hulls made the
canoe very stable.

Hanseatic cog
1350–1450.
Enclosed quarters. Traders
navigated with astrolabe.

Explorers and traders have sailed across the world in all kinds of ships. From the ancient trading boats, which relied on muscle and wind power, to the invention of the steamship, ship-building techniques and ways of navigating have changed dramatically. As boats became faster and better, explorers were able to journey farther. They discovered new lands and peoples, and opened up new trading routes. Slowly, the map of the world began to grow as land and sea borders were defined and claimed by different countries. The speed of travel also became important as traders competed for the limited number of markets around the world. The history of exploration and trade is the history of explorers and ships. These pages map the routes of some of the explorers in this book and show a few of the ships that took traders on their voyages.

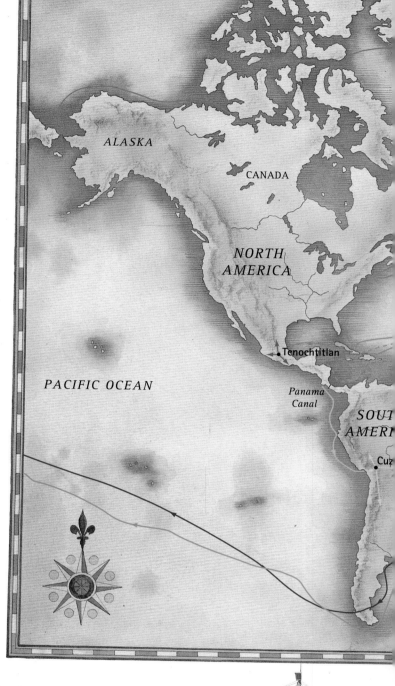

Caravel
1430–1520.
Streamlined and strengthened
by internal frame.
Able to venture into shallow
waters.

Zheng He's junk
Early to mid-15th century.
Big sails stiffened by bamboo
slats for support.
Zheng He navigated with
a magnetic compass.

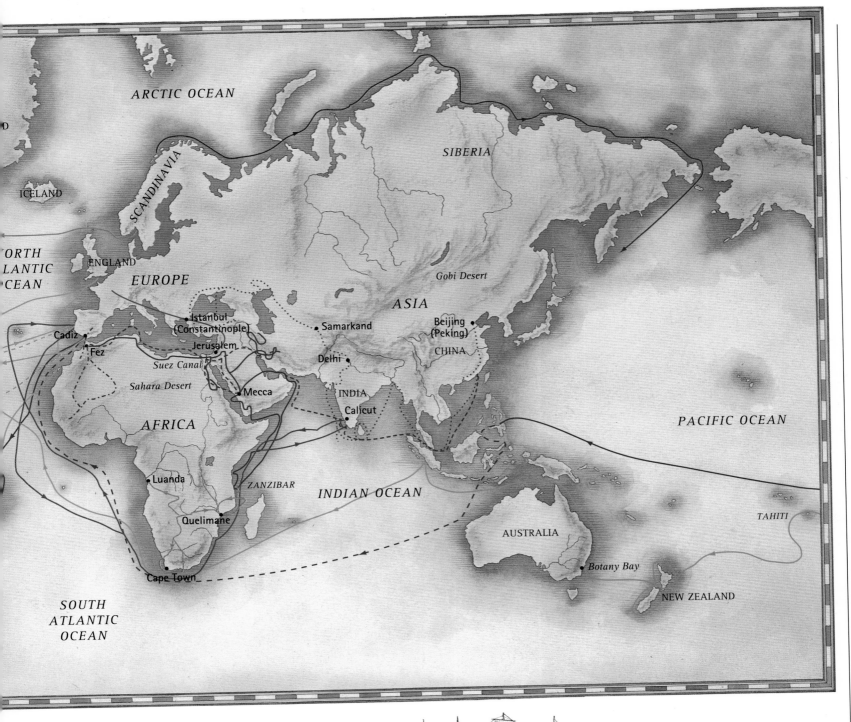

ARCTIC OCEAN

SIBERIA

ICELAND

SCANDINAVIA

NORTH ATLANTIC OCEAN

ENGLAND

EUROPE

ASIA

Gobi Desert

Istanbul (Constantinople)

Samarkand

Beijing (Peking)

Cadiz

Fez

Jerusalem

Delhi

CHINA

Suez Canal

Sahara Desert

Mecca

INDIA

Calicut

PACIFIC OCEAN

AFRICA

Luanda

ZANZIBAR

INDIAN OCEAN

Quelimane

AUSTRALIA

TAHITI

Cape Town

Botany Bay

SOUTH ATLANTIC OCEAN

NEW ZEALAND

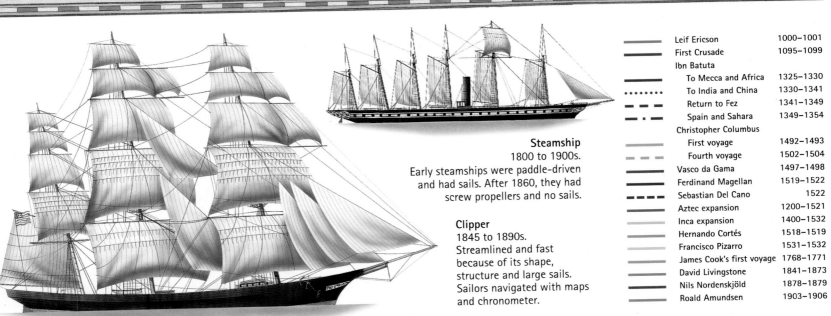

Steamship
1800 to 1900s.
Early steamships were paddle-driven and had sails. After 1860, they had screw propellers and no sails.

Clipper
1845 to 1890s.
Streamlined and fast because of its shape, structure and large sails. Sailors navigated with maps and chronometer.

Leif Ericson	1000–1001
First Crusade	1095–1099
Ibn Batuta	
To Mecca and Africa	1325–1330
To India and China	1330–1341
Return to Fez	1341–1349
Spain and Sahara	1349–1354
Christopher Columbus	
First voyage	1492–1493
Fourth voyage	1502–1504
Vasco da Gama	1497–1498
Ferdinand Magellan	1519–1522
Sebastian Del Cano	1522
Aztec expansion	1200–1521
Inca expansion	1400–1532
Hernando Cortés	1518–1519
Francisco Pizarro	1531–1532
James Cook's first voyage	1768–1771
David Livingstone	1841–1873
Nils Nordenskjöld	1878–1879
Roald Amundsen	1903–1906

Glossary

Incan god

amphitheater Usually a circular building where rows of seats rise up from a central open arena. In ancient Rome, gladiators fought each other and wild animals in amphitheaters while spectators watched and cheered.

Arabian Nights A collection of folk tales dating from the tenth century. The stories come from Arabia, Egypt, India, Persia and many other countries.

archaeologist Someone who studies the past by digging up the remains of ancient civilizations and analyzing everything he or she finds.

astrolabe A navigational instrument used by early sailors to measure the position of stars and planets to find out how far north or south they had traveled.

atoll A circular coral reef or string of coral islands that surround a lagoon. There are many atolls in the Pacific Ocean.

Aztecs The people who established a great empire in Mexico during the 1400s and early 1500s. Their civilization was very advanced, and they built huge cities. The Aztec Empire was destroyed by Spanish invaders.

barter To trade goods or services in exchange for other goods or services, rather than using money.

bubonic plague A contagious disease that is carried by flea-infested rats. It is also called the Black Death because people with the disease have spots of blood under the skin that turn black. It spread through Europe in the Middle Ages.

Buddhism One of the major religions in the world. It began in India more than 2,000 years ago and is based on the teachings of Siddhartha Gautama, who became known as the Buddha. Explorers and traders carried Buddhism eastwards as far as Japan.

caravel A sailing ship with two or three masts. The Spaniards and the Portuguese sailed in caravels in the fifteenth and sixteenth centuries.

carnelian A red or reddish-orange kind of quartz used as a gemstone in jewelry.

city-state An independent city that has its own laws and government. Athens and Rome were the most famous city-states in ancient times.

Turkish merchants

Jade pendant

Map of Drake's travels

civilization An advanced society that has cities and has invented writing. It has an organized system of government and law and high standards in arts, crafts and technology.

clippers Fast ships with narrow hulls and large sails on tall masts. They were built in the United States in the mid-1800s and were used on many trade routes.

cogs The type of trading ships used in Europe by the Hanseatic League in the 1300s.

cola nut A seed of the cola tree, which contains caffeine. Cola nuts were often used in medicines.

conquistadors From a Spanish word for adventurers or conquerors. It is used especially to describe the Spaniards who conquered the New World in the sixteenth century.

cuneiform A system of writing invented by the Sumerians and then used by later peoples of Mesopotamia. The word means wedge-shaped, and describes the shape of the characters used in cuneiform.

dhows Arab ships with triangular sails and one or two masts. Arab traders sailed along the coast in dhows hundreds of years ago. They are still used in the Middle East.

Eastern Hemisphere The part of the globe that contains Europe, Asia and Africa.

empire The people and territories under the rule of a single person or state. Great Britain, the Netherlands, France and other countries had trading empires throughout the world.

Far East The countries of East Asia, such as China, Japan and Indonesia.

flagship The main ship in a fleet of ships. The commander has his quarters there. The Santa Maria was Christopher Columbus's flagship.

flint A grayish-black form of quartz that was used by ancient peoples to make tools and weapons. It was often traded for other goods.

galleons Large sailing ships with three or more masts. They were used as warships and trading vessels by countries such as Spain from the fifteenth to the eighteenth centuries.

hieroglyphs The ancient Egyptian form of writing in which pictures or symbols represented sounds, objects and ideas.

ice age A period in the Earth's history when glaciers spread and ice covered large areas of some of the Earth's landmasses.

Incas The people who lived in Peru in South America from about 1100 to the 1530s. They had a great empire, which was destroyed by the Spaniards.

Industrial Revolution A process that began in Great Britain in the mid-1700s and spread to other parts of Europe and North America in the 1800s. It involved new methods of transport and new machines, driven by coal, electricity or other power sources.

junks Chinese ships with square sails.

knorrs Shallow-bottomed ships used by the Vikings to carry cargo.

lapis lazuli A brilliant blue mineral that is used as a gemstone.

longships The swift, sleek warships that carried invading parties of Vikings to western Europe.

Middle Ages The period of European history from about 1000 to the 1400s.

Mogul A member of the Muslim dynasty of Indian emperors that began ruling India in 1526.

monsoon winds Winds that change direction with the season. In Southeast Asia they blow from the southwest in summer and from the northeast in winter.

mutineers People who rebel against those who have authority over them. Sailors sometimes mutinied against their captains.

Near East Another term for the Middle East. It describes the countries round the eastern end of the Mediterranean Sea.

New World The term given to the Americas when these new continents were discovered in the Western Hemisphere.

oasis A fertile patch in a desert where water is available. Traders and travelers rested at oases on their journeys across the Sahara Desert.

obsidian A dark glass made by a volcanic explosion. It is formed when lava hardens quickly. Obsidian is sharp and cuts well. It was valuable to ancient peoples who made utensils from it. They traded for obsidian across long distances.

Old World The part of the world in the Eastern Hemisphere that was known before the Americas were discovered by Christopher Columbus. It was made up of Europe, Asia and Africa.

papyrus A kind of paper used by the ancient Egyptians. It was made from the papyrus plant.

pictographs Pictures or symbols that represent words. Pictographs were one of the earliest forms of writing.

pilgrim A person who makes a religious journey to a sacred place, such as Jerusalem or Mecca.

Punt An important trading country in the ancient world. It was particularly valued for its incense. Punt is the Egyptian name for the land, which was probably situated in what is now Somalia.

scurvy A disease, caused by lack of Vitamin C, which was common to early sailors. They did not have fresh fruit and vegetables on their long sea voyages. Captain Cook stopped his men getting scurvy by making them eat pickled cabbage.

shogun Originally a military title. It was used by the men who controlled the government of Japan from 1192 to 1867.

Spanish Armada The fleet of heavily armed warships sent by Philip II of Spain to attack England in 1588. The Spaniards were defeated in the English Channel.

Spice Islands A group of islands in the East that were the source of precious spices in the 1400s. Later, they became known as the Moluccas. Through the years, traders from many countries tried to gain control of these prized islands.

trade colony A settlement of merchants in a foreign land who trade with their home country.

Tuareg tribesmen The largest group of nomads living in the Sahara Desert. They herd camels, goats, sheep and cattle and move about finding pasture for their animals. They are sometimes called the Blue Men of the Desert because they wear robes that are dyed indigo and blue marks are often left on their skin.

Western Hemisphere The part of the world that contains the Americas.

Weaving cotton in India

Roman gladiators

Greek vase

Ancient weapons

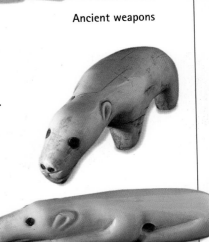

Ivory walruses

Index

Picture Credits

(t=top, b=bottom, l=left, r=right, c=center, F=front, C=cover, B=back, Bg=background)
Ad-Libitum, 35br, 36tl (S. Bowey). **AKG, London**, 11cr, 21tr, 63tcr (E. Lessing), 34tl (Metropolitan Museum of Art, New York), 14tl, 35tr, 36c, 38tl, 49tr. **Ancient Art & Architecture Collection**, 7tl, 11br, 12tr, 14cr, 23bc, 23bcr, 29br. **Ashmolean Museum, Oxford**, 8tl. **Auscape**, 19tr (K. Atkinson), 16bc (T. de Roy), 16cl (J.P. Ferrero), 13cr (M. Freeman). **Australian Museum**, 16tl. **Australian Picture Library**, 49br (J. Carnemolla), 10bl, 18/19t, 27bl, 29tl, 39tr, 41tl, 44tl, 53bl, 63cr (E.T. Archive), 12cr (E.T. Archive/Correr Museum Library, Venice), 56tr (D. & J. Heaton), 33tcr (L. Meier). **Black Star**, 57tc (J. Lopinot), 52bl (F. Ward). **The Bridgeman Art Library**, 20tl (Bibliotheque Nationale, Paris), 22bl (Bibliotheque Royale, Brussels), 21tl, 44bl, 46bc, 50bl, 63tr (British Library), 14tr, 23br (British Museum), 50bc (Christie's, London), 43tr, 44c (Fitzwilliam Museum, University of Cambridge), 20tc (The Louvre), 54c (National Maritime Museum, London), 10cl, 32cr (Nationalmuseet, Copenhagen), 44tr (O'Shea Gallery, London), 52br (Stapleton Collection), 42tc (Tower of London Armouries), 40bl, 63br (University of British Columbia), 33cl (University of Witwatersrand,

Johannesburg), 10tl. **C.M. Dixon**, 52bc. **The Granger Collection**, l, 6cr, 9tr, 15tr, 19cr, 23cl, 28cl, 28tr, 32tr, 38bc, 38cl, 40cl, 55br, 62bl. **Hutchison Library**, 24bl (C. Dodwell), 24bc (C. Hughes). **The Image Bank**, 36bl, 62tl (F. Hidalgo), 59tc (P. Kaehler), 59tr (M. Melford), 58cr (M. St. Gil). **The Mansell Collection**, 8bl. **Mary Evans Picture Library**, 22tl, 27cr, 36tr, 37tr, 41br, 43br, 45br, 46cl, 47br, 48tl, 49tl, 52cr. **National Geographic Society**, 26tr (B. Silverman). **North Wind Picture Archives**, 27tl, 33tl. **Orion Press**, 54bl. **Robert Harding Picture Library**, 50tl (M. Joseph), 32tl (P. Scholey), 19tc (J.H.C. Wilson), 7cl (A. Woolfit). **Wave Productions**, 16bl (O. Strewe). **Werner Forman Archive**, 31br (Asiatische-Sammlung Collection, Bad Wildungen, Germany), 6tr, 17cr, 54tl, 62cl (The Louvre), 8tcl (The Louvre), 18tl (Courtesy Sotheby's, London), 14cl (Statens Historiska Museum, Stockholm).

Illustration Credits

Paul Bachem, 4tl, 18/19b, 30/31b, 30cl, 48/49c. **Kenn Backhaus**, 28/29c. **Nick Farmer/Brihton Illustration**, 40/41c, 46/47c, 46bl. **Chris Forsey**, 2, 6/7c, 6tr, 23-26c, 54/55c, 63bcr. **Tony Gibbons/Bernard Thornton

Artists, UK, 3, 16/17c, 30bl, 60l, 60b, 61b. **Adam Hook/Bernard Thornton Artists, UK**, 4bl, 8/9c, 38/39c. **Christa Hook/Bernard Thornton Artists, UK**, 12/13c, 13c, 34/35c, 34tr, 34bl. **Janet Jones**, 44/45c. **Steinar Lund/Garden Studio**, 14/15c, 15cr. **Martin Macrae/Folio**, 4/5b, 10/11c, 36/37c. **Darren Pattenden/Garden Studio**, 52/53c. **Oliver Rennert**, 7br, 22/27c. **John Richards**, 5tr, 32/33b, 56/57b, 57br, 58/59c, 58bl. **Sharif Tarabay/Garden Studio**, 5br, 20/21c, 50/51c, 50cl. **C. Winston Taylor**, 42/43c, 42bl. **Rod Westblade**, 32tr, 57tl, 57tr, endpapers, icons.

Maps

Steve Trevaskis, Mark Watson

Cover Credits

Australian Picture Library, FCtl (E.T. Archive). Tony Gibbons/Bernard Thornton Artists, UK, BCbr. The Image Bank, BCtl (F. Hidalgo), Bg (B. Roussel). Martin Macrae/Folio, FCc. Werner Forman Archive, FCtr (Courtesy Sotheby's, London).